GW00670551

Flint Wave

Jon Brooks

Photographs by Moya Burns

Grosvenor House
Publishing Limited

This book is published by
Grosvenor House Publishing Ltd
Link House
140 The Broadway, Tolworth, Surrey, KT6 7HT.
www.grosvenorhousepublishing.co.uk

A CIP record for this book
is available from the British Library

ISBN 978-1-83975-483-8

Dedicated to Moya, Alex, Justine, and Rowen

Contents

The Cake   1

The Woodland Watcher   3

Mourn as Day Dies   4

Not Waking but Dreaming   5

My Words are Offerings   7

And then I Slept   14

Sunken Circle   15

Up Past the Windmill   16

Firle Beacon   17

The Path Corner   18

Silent Hawthorn bows   19

The Sun reflected   20

Soft Words bring Sleep   27

Circular Path   30

Old Black Trench Coat   32

More than I   34

Fallen Fallers   36

That my Body is a Ruin   37

As yet Unmade Beds   38

Black Bell   45

The Coast Drifter   47

The Wave Painter   48

The Riddle One   49

The Riddle Two   50

The Riddle Three   51

The Last Train Leaves   52

—

The Cake

To sit with peacock cry
drink tea dark chocolate cake
watched by hills around us
yellow grass growing about
our wrought iron seats.
And the peacock cried
and the fox barked
and the pheasant ran
across the chalk lane.

The figure floated
over deep shadowed pond
her hair so long it rippled
green dark weed on reflecting surface.
We drank ate sang
in still fading haze
through long shadow sunset.

Ambling up white chalk lane
carved twisted plaited gulley
scarred by timeless hill streams.
Cow parsley common yarrow
cuckoo flower dog rose
goatsbeard and cowslip
heady to fill our senses.

Sparkle of rays through trees
high hills hide soft sun
till gilt leaves filled with light.
We followed a lazy pace
with our small gold dog
down white chalk lane
while garlands obscured
empty wrought iron seats
now in soft shade.

The Woodland Watcher

Yet more I loved when young than simple play
than barefoot ascend the canopy high
through distant woodland in haze to survey
sat silent searching the shadows pass by.
No storm could shake the form with fingers clung
entwined with bark no rain nor wind succeed
sat raven rook old songs eternal sung
laced limbs spiral springing from forest seed.
Where once I sat now with earth sunken lie
entwined with time torment deathless decay
done dark damp earth I hear silent sigh
cavern canopy daze summerlong play.
For I watched as light changed the days
the distant woodland and the distant haze.

Mourn as Day Dies

Mourn as day dies for moon is born
shadows glide over guiding stone
silent spirit flees dark fore dawn
slip scorned winters wind alone
storm blanched sea born land bound bone,
chalk white chasten raven replete
feel shadows flee beneath my feet.

That once clung beauty twice truth
now shadows slip away beneath
deed of the brave or dream of youth
yet praise that which others bequeath
lest leave the silence and the wreath,
colour the world my eyes create
hear the sound and taste food I ate.

So, mourn as day dies in moons haze
the rise the roll of squally seas
lost senses in dark winter ways
spiral path the mist past deceives
the still white frost the froze stone leaves,
touch the shadows that were senses
grieve not comfort felt commences.

Not Waking but Dreaming

Fearless night long winter darkness
night canopy of celestial
dreams - not waking but dreaming.
Gliding into ice-bound waters
darkened shadows of seals and whales
ice feathered hail dives the ocean,
my frosted fingers turn the tiller
my frozen eyes turn to shoreless sea.

Mist lost shadow of silent stone
lichen lined whiten hoar frost
dawn - not waking but dreaming.
Calling visit sea-mist voyage
cold snow moon with howling voices
grey sarsen black flint and white chalk,
silent stone surrounds wrenched spirit
white whisper haze echoes eternal.

Silver brook over shadowed brow
sleet blizzard obscures secret deep
sleep - not waking but dreaming.
Foot falls through thousand solstice
charred ash alter burnt brittle bone
white chalk timeless voices pathway,
spoken breeze spread across the hillside
spins earth spiral within waking dream.

My Words are Offerings

My words are offerings to you
small stones to turn in your hand
textures to touch to place on a shelf
on garden wall or at the gate.

My words are whispers in the wind
lacing the landscape with longing
journey following lost footpaths
we forgot and now reclaim.

My words are lyrics to be sung
by black-winged birds ravens rooks
an old orator defiant
sat in the distant leafless tree.

My words are images of magic
with an outstretched ochre hand
on a dark fire lit dancing frieze
silent silhouettes animate.

My words are poems to be read
in a circle or quietly in bed.

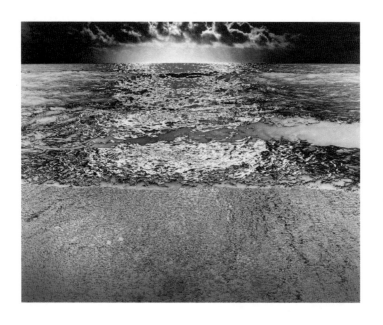

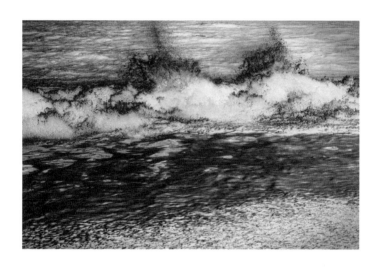

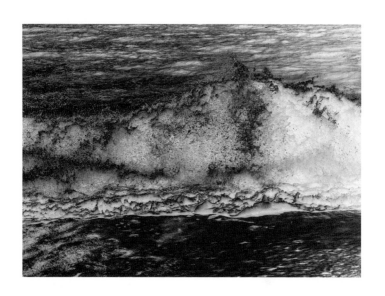

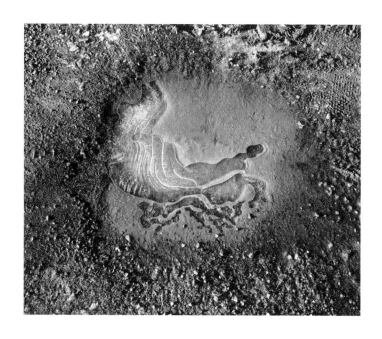

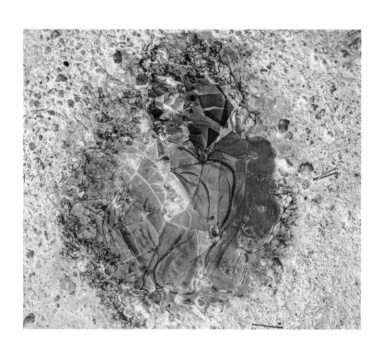

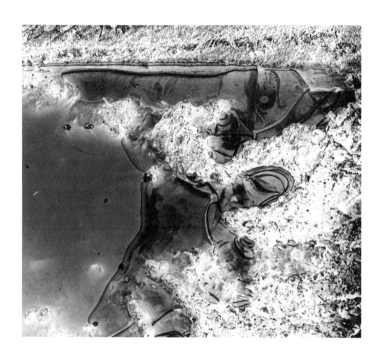

And then I Slept

And then I slept
in briar canopied hollow
shadow pierce speckled dust light wings, and
glow crumbling chalk release dark flint
that stole gold summer light.
And as I watch the stone shadow
move silent across hallowed place.

And as I slept
in tree root cave shelter shadowed
fungi lichen moss pollen seed, and
white bone washed winterbourne stream
blood berry-stained snow.
And as I watch chalk fall away
the unfettered flint now remains.

Sunken Circle

So spoke sunken circle to me
of my fate destiny,
if not I a listener be
earth bound eternity.

Wind voices warn on longest night
sea sweet swirl moonlit mist,
now filled with summerlong bright light
fade gentle now sun kissed.

So fate to me unknown no more
time slows to timeless pace,
to be is that was once before
silence still sacred place.

Up Past the Windmill

Footfall shadow falling forward
poem metre marks chalk white page
boneless foot falls on bone chalk spine
while a silent glider sails by.

Shortest steepest soon lightheaded
foot falls on flint unchained from chalk
see you sit and eat a sandwich
so soft slow wind then sends me by.

Firle Beacon

Dark blueness not dark darkness night
our spirits breath in time out time
less time time less till earth till dawn
slope zig-zag slope path chalk bone white.
Light whiteness is light lightness sight
our spirits view before before
blue red red beams set sun set moon
climb tack back climb chalk bone night light.

The Path Corner

Turn the path corner
in the summerlong dawn mist
in still timeless gaze.

Silent in still haze
rise calm swirl of high white mist
white chalk path dissolves.

Lie in fadeless glow
breathe out darkness and in time
reveal passing night.

The dead quiet mist
echoes burial voices
and mourning murmur.

Silent Hawthorn bows

Silent hawthorn bows
sensing the weight of the crows
melancholy stare.

Roil river swirl sea
curl and coil by edge of shore
not knowingly there.

View seven cliffs glow
hear pebbles washed by the waves
mirrored in river.

Stand at fold of hills
behold bend in the river
sense the shore at sea.

The Sun reflected

The sun reflected
off derelict grey wet roof
lights page of wisdom.

Water running down
onto streaky clean window
focusses my eye.

A flock of pigeons
land in the bare ash swaying
and quietly sit.

All the golden leaves
of the silver birch falling
one lone green leaf stays.

The bubble of soup
from the kitchen fills my thoughts
I try to study.

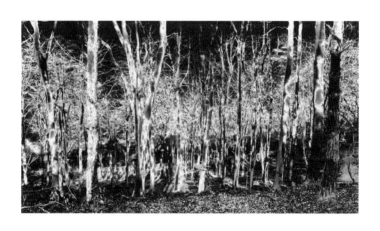

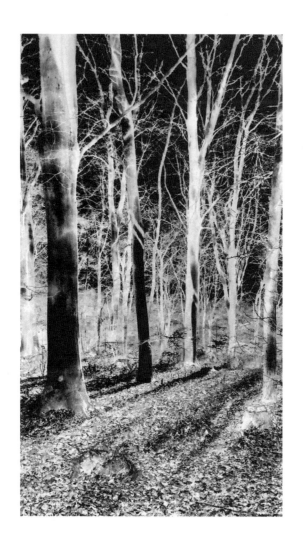

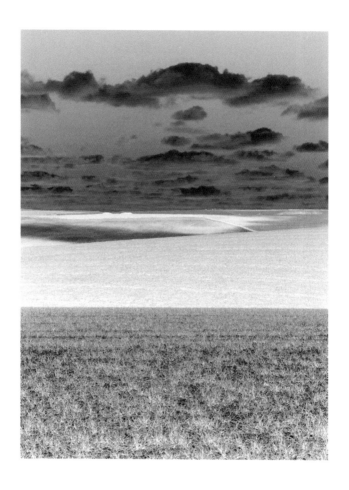

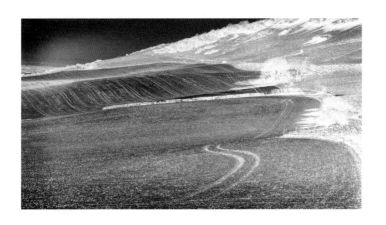

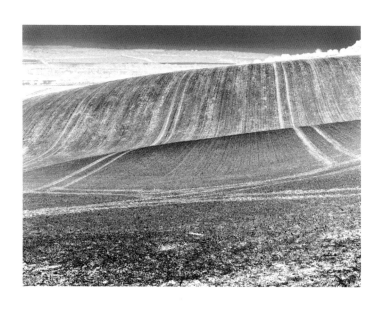

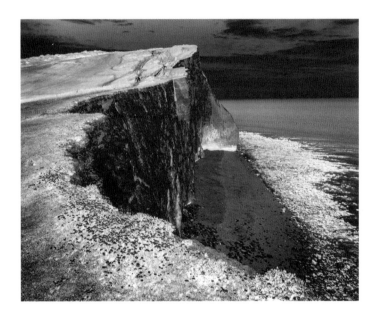

Soft Words bring Sleep

Soft words bring sleep
breath blown wind
zig zag tunnel time
sweep mournful sound
hurled from heights
channel chalk cliff
swirl turning tide
pull pebbles undertow
shoes left onshore
lifted by white waves.

Winged wanderers
criss cross spiral orbits
repeat ring cry
shores sorrow song
silent sad mourning
storm airborne
sensed sounds
off far offshore
blue scarf flew
tugged 'n tore.

Chalk face facing
hazy curl of cloud
slip shore shoulder
tack back high hill
that still space
calm swirl
flowing fields
not moving mist
glance into glare
half turn to talk.

Moon shroud
glancing beam
swirl shoreline
shaking wind
eager eyes
glance at going
dark and
light mist
as you walk waves
wash fleeing feet.

Spoken like song
sung across shore
brought by breeze
moments mist
where river met sea
salt stinging
splashing
timeless tug of tide
glancing stare
touch sea at shore.

Whisper wind's
erring echo
flowing feelings
outstretch over
taught emptiness
edge touch edge
finely floating
silent silhouette,
words we all hear
our soft solace.

Circular Path

Fly my feet fly by the whorled wind
echoing voices uncoil lines
the gold dog's fur furled in the breeze
white chalk paths flow across hillside.

Echoing voices uncoil lines
back to witness lost beginning
white chalk paths flow across hillside
spiralling into timeless breeze.

Back to witness lost beginning
whitening curled mist unscroll
spiralling into timeless breeze
spoken before in border lands.

Whitening curled mist unscroll
touch before atop the high hill
spoken before in border lands
recoil our feet do dance again.

Touch before atop the high hill
in the still calm haze of nights breath
recoil our feet do dance again
all fall slowly in evening call.

In the still calm haze of nights breath
wing feathers lift drifting glide by
all fall slowly in evening call
celestial beam radial bridge.

Wing feathers lift drifting glide by
hid pathways sleep in spiral snow
celestial beam radial bridge
decay darkly lost dance renews.

Hid pathways sleep in spiral snow
bone white drift still silent landscape
decay darkly lost dance renews
murmur loved voices guiding.

Bone white drift still silent landscape
the gold dog's fur furled in the breeze
murmur loved voices guiding
fly my feet fly by the whorled wind.

Old Black Trench Coat

Catch the moon with a yearning hand
speckled light rise tween the leaves,
drop white beams on snow covered sand
bright mist kiss waves in the breeze.
Then I glimpse you still and calm
your old black coat over your arm.

Timeless in silent bluebell glade
hid by shadow in bright sun,
now deep autumn leaves light fade
winters long sleep now begun.
Then I glimpse in shaded lane
your old black coat soaked in the rain.

Sat upon moonlit island rock
calm star light with lonely sail,
ascend white cliff pathway unlock
drifting voices reclaim trail.
Then I glimpse over the rise
your old black coat against the sky.

Fade luminous white lost image
rising light with dying sun,
echo murmurs paying homage
step on pathway we begun.
Then I glimpse fore the painting
in your old black coat, you waiting.

More than I

Haste
hasten to me,
leap up
leap to catch your
silhouette cut out blank eclipse,
shimmer sands spring fresh rivulets
to the sea.
More than I
had gotten more than I put in,
more than you
had gotten more than you put in.

Bound
bound up the hill,
tied to
tied to the sea
laughing fills arching light night high,
swirling wind echoing whispers
in the sky.
More than I
had gotten more than I put in,
more than you
had gotten more than you put in.

Slept
then as we slept,
woken
as still dreaming
feather flying spirit dark dawn,
wrenched spirit reach shoreless wave
in dreams.
More than I
had gotten more than I put in,
more than you
had gotten more than you put in.

Fallen Fallers

Fallen fallers in the fermenting mush
blue black darkness filling the garden haze
I searched for fallers with a broken brush.

I planted plants but I was in a rush
had not learnt to understand ways and days
fallen fallers in the fermenting mush.

That then mattered most was lost in the crush
cloud moon offered no clue to lost pathways
I searched for fallers with a broken brush.

Linger as grey light falls with the song thrush
dark damp earth eaten swallows and decays
fallen fallers in the fermenting mush.

I push away from the now pleading hush
leaned into my own sighing and dismays
I searched for fallers with a broken brush.

I fell fallen now mush now green now lush
regained one of the gardens old displays
fallen fallers in the fermenting mush
I searched for fallers with a broken brush.

That My Body is a Ruin

That my body is a ruin
of the spirit now wrenched fly
o'er dark forgotten forests
touch black feather white bared fang.
On cold temple stone once joyous
ivy columns now entwined
hoar frost frozen moss marble
ruin glistens rain dark dawn.

In celestial shoreless seas
breath without breath
bread without bread
body without body
in celestial shoreless seas.

I dreamed the darkness of the dawn
lived yet silent winter still moon
ice cold storm seas carried to shores
lost to eternal turning tides.
Awaken to dark light lantern
silver beam celestial compass
alight bright bridge white chalk pathway
spirit finds your guiding beacon.

As yet Unmade Beds

I weave down the crushed corridor
in an old wonky wheelchair,
the clear glass door opens open
the gold dust creating a haze.
With the torn plastic covering
flap newly rain drenched scaffolding,
now filled with feelings.
Shading the once light now dark light
pungent with burnt pizza burnt bread
mixed chemicals and muted pain.

Pushed down empty corridors
in a wonky old wheelchair,
rising ramp of frosted windows
guided pathways through lost gardens.
Now lie quite flat now lie quite still
worn metal piercing worn out muscle,
now filled with feelings.
Silent plants with light refracted
blinding emotion now dark light
frosted prism blinking burnt pain.

Next to some as yet unmade beds
in an old wonky wheelchair,
with murmurs of weightless voices
someone draws a moonlit curtain.
Silver dust settles on bracelets
of wire wrapped around my wrists,
now filled with feelings.
Captured characters from my folktale
acceptance of dark not now light
drift down dimly lit corridors.

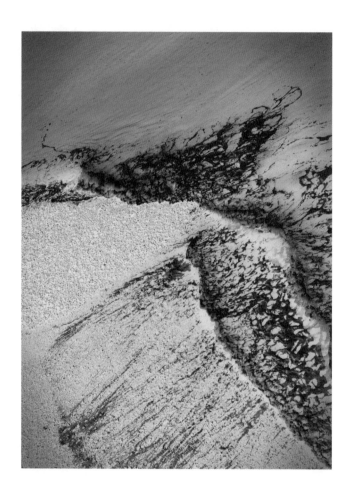

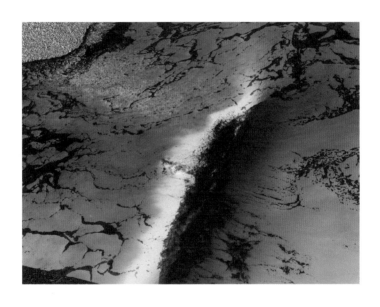

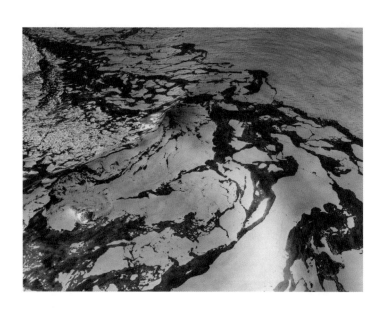

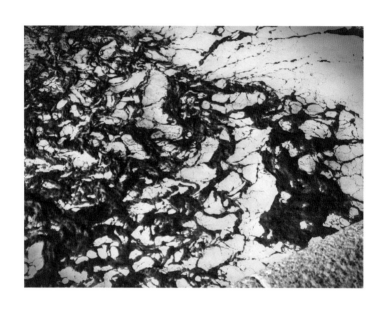

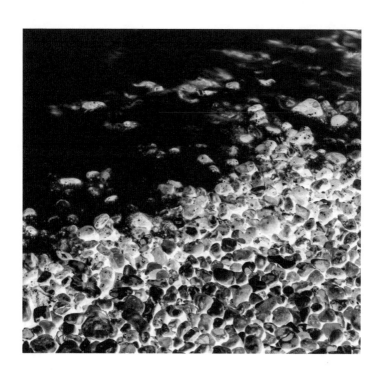

Black Bell

So! bellow black bell
call to standing stone
sat rook on pious ruin
now fly atop leafless crown.

Silent shadows emerge
shroud in silver smoke
bearing cross and
burning torch to process.

Through narrow streets
friends of friends arm 'n arm
gold givers smugglers
sea bound buccaneer.

We own the streets
we prove to power
we will hand down
that which
we have been given.

Echo ancient voices
as stone reflect fire
swirl smoke swithun
turn torch lit twitten.

Our cry is a calling
we rest to remember
in silent solemnity
we march in memory.

Fire burns wood
water quenches fire
earth dries water
smoke swirls in air.

Ash is borne by wind
scattered in silent street
we melt our fetters
that clung like a frost.

At sunrise silent
is the black bell.

The Coast Drifter

I sail with a sea breeze by coasts in the morning
the dawn of the summerlong birth of eternal,
I'm sailing alone with the wolf and the walrus
the seabird song keeps me and guides with a chorus.

I live by the fishing in summer where seals swim
the Finns fight the Norse who now cross the wild
    ice-stream,
Coast Sami help fishing and trading that I can buy
they layout their goods on the ice below the sky.

The sea is not frozen the warmth is forgiving
the wind is now blowing the waves crest below me,
on land you await I'm now lost you are thinking
the rain makes you unhappy the ice is now freezing.

I travel for hundreds of miles in the landscape
with rivers of ice race wild horses are raiding,
far into the realm of the gold and the silver
I return to the sea-ice with gifts for ring-giver.

The Wave Painter

Ahoy! Away - a hoist of sail
a bosun hitch - a boat untied
anchors aweigh - all oars engaged
I painted waves - pining the sea.

Erce mother - earth awakens
Gods night candle - calling the seas
steering sail ships - stairs guiding light
alight bright bridge - celestial beam.

The spirit soars - sails touch my wings
walking in seas - whale's domain
forces unleash - frost fingers sting
spirit frozen - man's form shamed.

Kings gaze on us - light gates open
ancestor's breath - announces land
a ring-whorled ship - with gold treasure
risen ashore - by Kings right hand.

The Riddle One

I am born with many but singled out,
learn a new name and a language.
I find anything without seeing it,
eat all day without being full,
run all day without tiring.
I can sleep in the snow, swim in the sea,
jump over hedges, run underground.
I chase anything which moves,
then sleep by the fire and dream.
You know my nature, now guess my name.

Answer: a dog.

The Riddle Two

With me you glide across the spine of the waves,
the army of clouds and rain cannot deter me.
Move out of strife driven by the struggle of streams,
under the helm of a front guided by a current.
Without me you languish neither backward nor forward,
without me the echo of emptiness
moves across the landscape.
Without me your hands blister with effort,
your frost fettered feet feel the cold night.
You know my power, know my name.

Answer: the wind.

The Riddle Three

I am unique but each has one,
you cannot see me but know me instantly,
I cannot be caged but can be captured.
I inform you of the knowledge of the world,
take you on innumerable journeys.
Comfort you, call you, command you,
conjure your imagination.
I call your name, can you call mine?

Answer: a voice.

The Last Train leaves

Bright yellow beach huts glow in last suns ray
low light moves up the white building walkway
grey landscape as the shadow growing long
alone now as everyone is long gone,
cold white wind carries the sound of a tune
the last train leaves - I think pretty soon.

Distant lights come on to challenge the dusk
I pursued the path that perish and crush
the gold dog fur furled by the sea air
watching the distance in a melancholy stare,
silver grey huts glow in the rising moon
the last train leaves - I think pretty soon.

Strangers wave as they pass across the street
I try to nod to everyone I meet
just to stare now I don't know what to say
my limbs near numb now my skins going grey,
sitting on the old worn wooden pontoon
the last train leaves - I think pretty soon.

If the sea does not get me the old grog will
it cushions the fall that's not a big spill
spokes are rusty on my wonky wheelchair
moons clouding over there's rain in the air,
the last trains leaving - see lights in the gloom
don't worry, I'll be home pretty soon.

END.

CPSIA information can be obtained at www.ICGtesting.com
Printed in the USA
BVIW121209310321
603847BV00012B/55/J

9 781839 754838